Contents

Welcome

1 ✏️ Match and trace.

1  2 3 4

a c

b  d

Hello. I'm
__Beth__.

Hello. I'm
__Cody__.

Hello.
My name's
__Waldo__.

Hello.
My name's
__Harry__.

2 ✏️ ✏️ **Trace. Then colour.**

1 **2** **3** **4**

blue   red   yellow   green

3 🎧 1:08 ✏️ **Listen and ✓. Then colour.**

1
☐ yellow
✓ blue

2
☐ red
☐ green

3
☐ yellow
☐ red

4
☐ green
☐ blue

4 Read and trace.

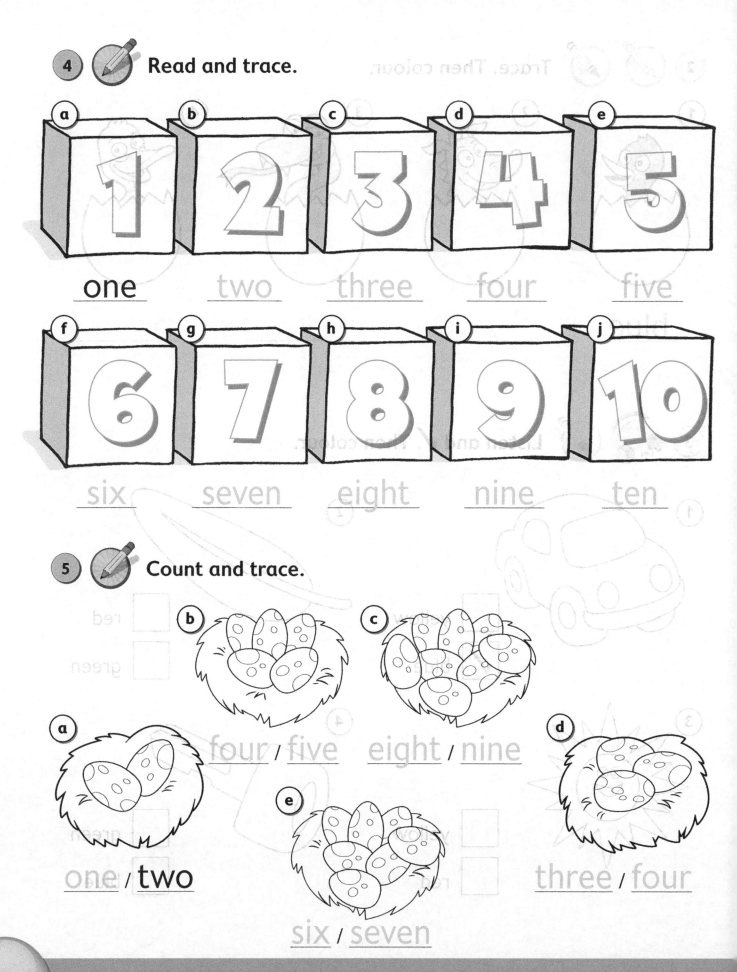

a 1 one
b 2 two
c 3 three
d 4 four
e 5 five

f 6 six
g 7 seven
h 8 eight
i 9 nine
j 10 ten

5 Count and trace.

a one / two

b four / five

c eight / nine

d three / four

e six / seven

6 ✏️ ✏️ **Colour. Then match and trace.**

1   **2**   **3**   **4**

a His   **b** Her   **c** His   **d** His

name's Waldo.   name's Beth.   name's Cody.   name's Harry.

7 ✏️ ✏️ **Circle and colour.**

1   **2**

(His / Her) balloon is blue.   (His / Her) balloon is red.

8 🎧 1:15 ✏️ **Read. Then listen and number.**

(a) ☐ count

(b) 1 sit down

(c) ☐ stand up

(d) ☐ listen

(e) ☐ open your book

(f) ☐ close your book

(g) ☐ look

(h) ☐ wave goodbye

9 ✏️ Follow and colour.

1	red
2	yellow
3	blue
4	green

ⓐ **2**
ⓑ **5**
ⓒ **7**
ⓓ **9**

10 ✏️ Read and match.

1   **2**   **3**   **4**

ⓐ Goodbye Cody!

ⓑ Hello Cody. My name's Harry.

ⓒ Hello. My name's Cody.

ⓓ Goodbye Harry!

1 ✏️ 🖍️ **Trace and colour.**

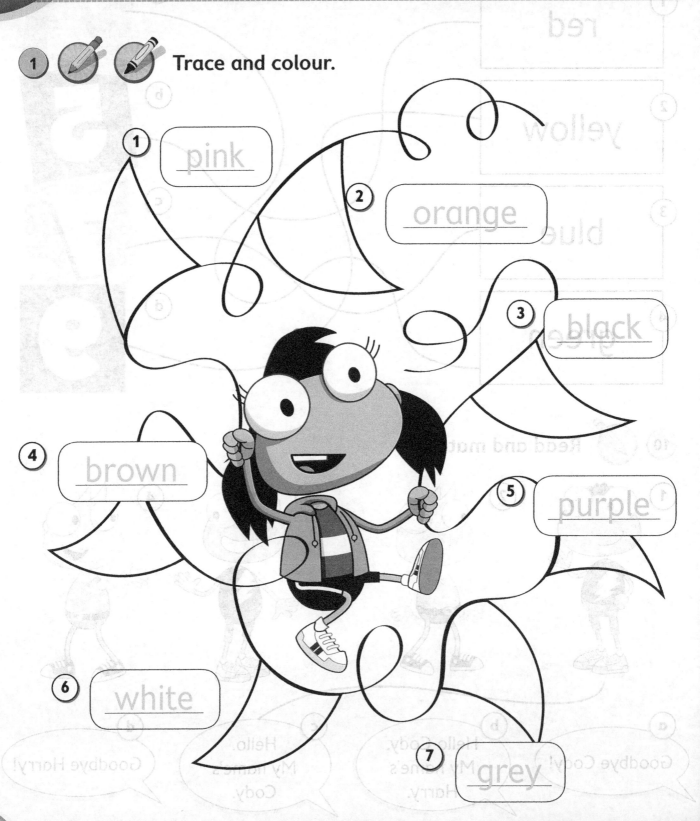

1 pink

2 orange

3 black

4 brown

5 purple

6 white

7 grey

2 **Listen and number.**

3 **Look and trace. Then colour.**

a I'm _four_. My favourite colour is _orange_.

b I'm _seven_. My favourite colour is _grey_.

c I'm _nine_. My favourite colour is _pink_.

d I'm _ten_. My favourite colour is _purple_.

④ 🖊 **Match. Then trace.**

1
2
3
4
5
6
7
8

a — stamp
b — climb
c — run
d — jump
e — dance
f — clap
g — hop
h — walk

5 **Read and trace. Then colour.**

1

What colour is it?

It's ___purple___ .

2

What colour is it?

It's ___orange___ .

3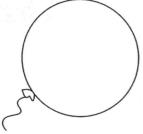

What colour ___is it___ ?

It's blue.

4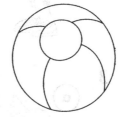

What colour is it?

___It's___ yellow.

5

Is it red?

___No___ , it isn't. It's pink.

6

Is it brown?

___Yes___ , it is.

7

Is it white?

No, ___it isn't___ . It's green.

8

Is it black?

Yes, ___it is___ .

6 🎧 1:30 ✏️ Listen and circle. Then colour.

1

a    b

2

a    b

3

a    b

7 ✏️ Look and ✓ or ✗.

VALUES

1

2

8 ✏️ **Read the words and circle.**

9 🎧 1:34 ✏️ **Listen to the sounds and circle the letters.**

1 t p a s

2 p s t a

3 s t p a

4 t a s p

10 🎧 1:35 ✏️ **Listen and write the letters.** a p s t

1 ___t___ **2** _____ **3** _____ **4** _____

11 🎧 1:36 ✏️ **Listen and circle the words.**

1 sat / at **2** tap / pat **3** at / pat **4** pat / sat

12 Match. Then trace.

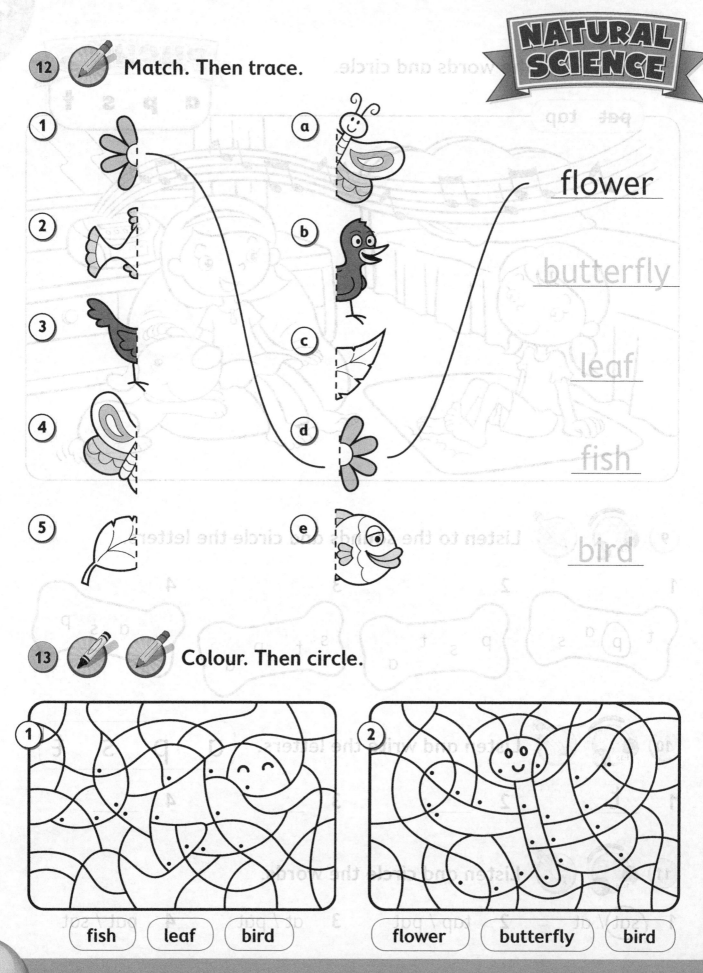

1
2
3
4
5

a
b
c
d
e

flower

butterfly

leaf

fish

bird

13 Colour. Then circle.

1

2

| fish | leaf | bird |

| flower | butterfly | bird |

Wider World

14 **Trace and match.**

a

1 birthday cake

b

2 balloon

c

3 present

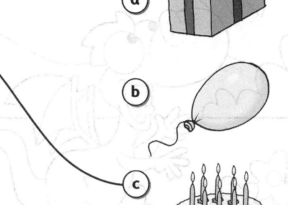

15   **Draw and colour. Then write.**

HAPPY BIRTHDAY

1 How old are you? _____.

2 How many balloons? _____.

3 What colour is the present? _____.

16 **Read and colour.**

1	black
2	brown
3	blue
4	purple
5	pink
6	orange
7	green
8	grey

 17 **Look and circle.**

1 What's your name? My name's Harry. / His name's Cody.

2 How old are you? It's six. / I'm six.

3 What's your favourite colour? My favourite colour is blue. /
His favourite colour is blue.

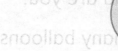 

18   **Read and trace. Then colour.**

Hello. ¹ My name's Ana.

² I'm seven.

My favourite colour

³ is pink.

Look! A ⁴ pink butterfly!

Goodbye!

19   **Draw and write.**

Hello. My name's

_____.

I'm _____.

My favourite colour is

_____.

Goodbye!

2 At school

1 Draw. Then trace.

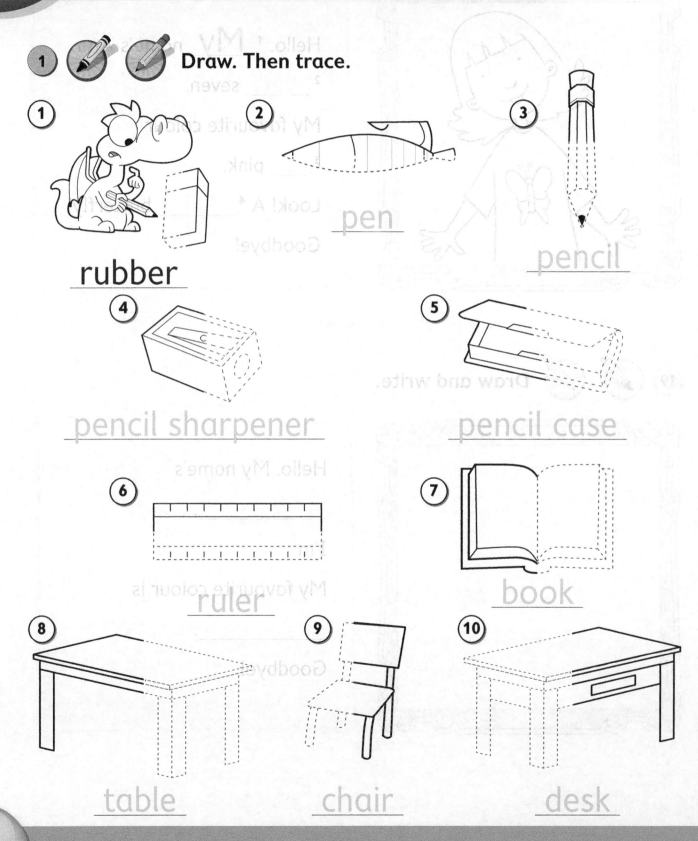

1 rubber

2 pen

3 pencil

4 pencil sharpener

5 pencil case

6 ruler

7 book

8 table

9 chair

10 desk

2 Read and match. Then colour.

1. It's a pencil sharpener. It's green.

a

2. It's a table. It's brown.

b

3. It's a chair. It's orange.

c

4. It's a rubber. It's red and blue.

d

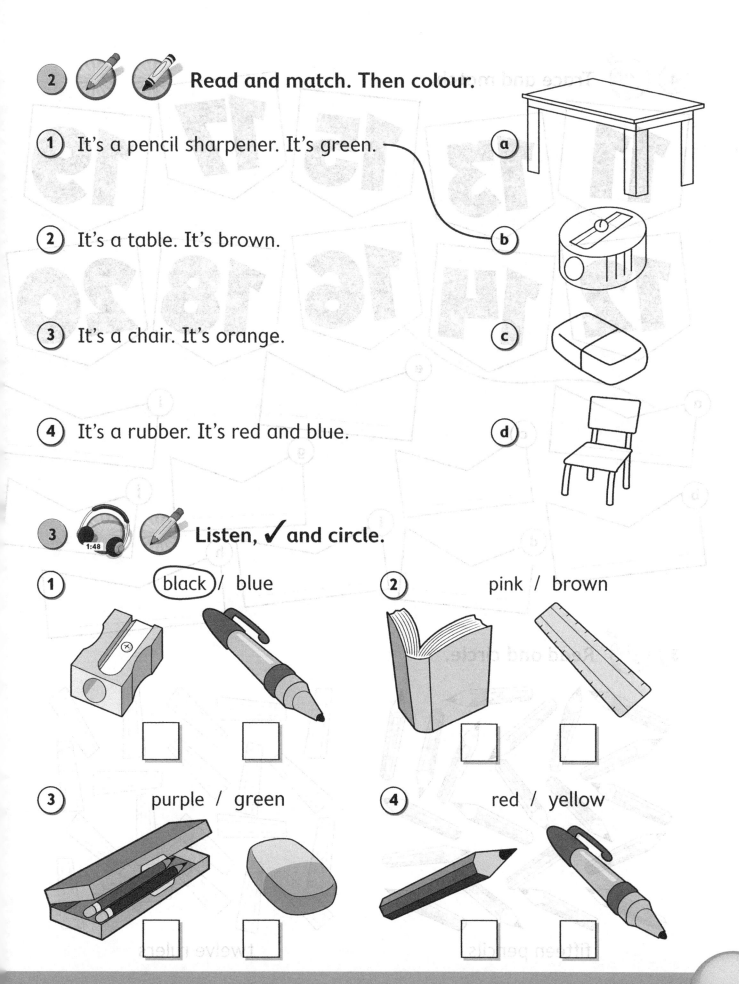

3 Listen, ✓ and circle.

1. (black) / blue

2. pink / brown

3. purple / green

4. red / yellow

4 Trace and match.

11   13   15   17   19

12   14   16   18   20

a sixteen

b eighteen

c eleven

d twenty

e fourteen

f thirteen

g fifteen

h seventeen

i nineteen

j twelve

5 Read and circle.

fifteen pencils

twelve rulers

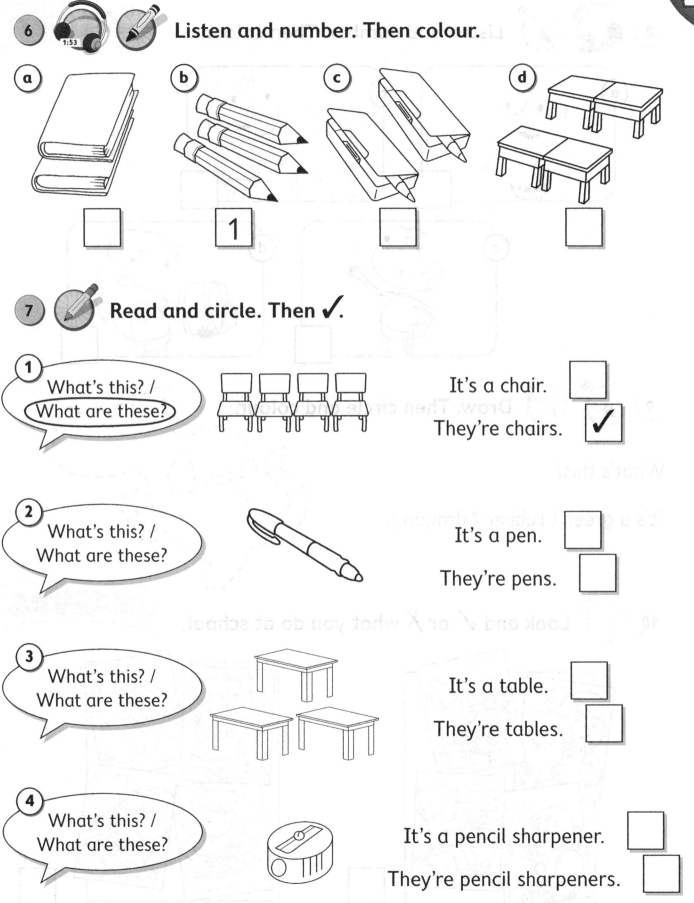

6 **Listen and number. Then colour.**

1:53

a

b **1**

c

d

7 **Read and circle. Then ✓.**

1 What's this? / (What are these?)

It's a chair.

They're chairs. ✓

2 What's this? / What are these?

It's a pen.

They're pens.

3 What's this? / What are these?

It's a table.

They're tables.

4 What's this? / What are these?

It's a pencil sharpener.

They're pencil sharpeners.

8 Listen and number. Then colour.

9   Draw. Then circle and colour.

What's this?

It's a green (rubber / dragon).

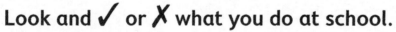

10 Look and ✔ or ✗ what you do at school.

11 Read the words and circle.

~~dip~~   man   nap   pan

12 Listen to the sounds and circle the letters.

1:59

1
a d m n

2
d m i p

3
a i n t

4
p d i t

13 Listen and write the letters.

1:60

d i ~~m~~ n

1 __m__   2 ____   3 ____   4 ____

14 Listen and circle the words.

1:61

1 (sit) / dip   2 dad / am   3 dip / man   4 it / sit

15 Match and trace.

piano   guitar   drum   violin

16 Read and circle.

It's a ((guitar) / drum).   It's a (piano / violin).   It's a (piano / drum).

17 **Trace and match.**

1 __school__

2 __playground__

3 __teacher__

4 __pupil__

a

b

c

d

18 **Look, count and trace.**

1 How many tables can you see?   **two** / three

2 How many chairs can you see?   five / six

3 How many pencils can you see?   one / three

19   **Read and match. Then colour.**

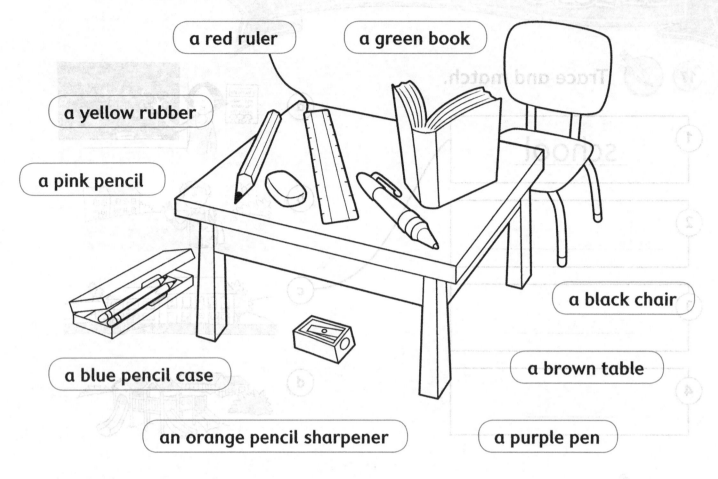

a red ruler

a green book

a yellow rubber

a pink pencil

a black chair

a brown table

a blue pencil case

an orange pencil sharpener

a purple pen

20 **Join the dots. Then read and circle.**

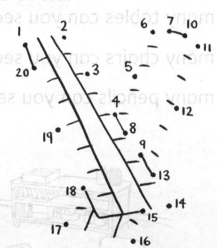

(What's this?)/ What are these?

It's a book. / They're books.

What's this? / What are these?

It's a ruler. / They're rulers.

Read and circle. Then colour.

¹ (**This** / These) is my desk.

² (This / **These**) are my books.

They're red and blue.

And ³ (this / these) is my

pencil case. It's pink.

Can you see two pens?

They're green.

 Draw your desk and write.

This is my _____.

These are my _____.

They're _____.

And this is my _____.

It's _____.

Can you see _____?

They're _____.

3 My family

1 ✏️ **Trace and number.**

1 mum   **2** dad   **3** sister   **4** brother

This is my __family__.

5 grandad

6 granny

7 friend

Find and colour. Then read and circle.

This is my (mum / (friend)).

((He's) / She's) ((nine) / ten).

This is my (granny / sister).

(He's / She's) (seven / eight).

 Trace and match.

1 How old is he? __He's eight__ .

2 How old is she? __She's seven__ .

3 How old is she? __She's five__ .

4 How old is he? __He's ten__ .

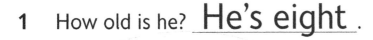

4   **Look and write.**

| vet | pilot | doctor | dentist |
| cook | artist | farmer | dancer |

(cook is crossed out)

 1

 2

 3

 4

cook

 5

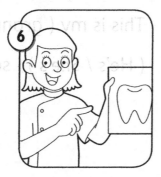 6

 7

 8

_____   _____

5 **Read and circle.**

My (mum / dad)
is a (farmer / doctor).

My (mum / dad)
is a (pilot / teacher).

6 **Match. Then read and circle.**

1 Is she a doctor? (Yes, she is. / No, she isn't.)

2 Is she an artist? (Yes, she is. / No, she isn't.)

3 Is he a vet? (Yes, he is. / No, he isn't.)

4 Is he a teacher? (Yes, he is. / No, he isn't.)

7  **Listen and ✓. Then write.**

| ~~cook~~   doctor |
| artist   pilot |

☐ Yes, he is.
✓ No, he isn't.
He's a __cook__ .

☐ Yes, she is.
☐ No, she isn't.
She's a _____ .

☐ Yes, he is.
☐ No, he isn't.
He's an _____ .

☐ Yes, she is.
☐ No, she isn't.
She's a _____ .

8 ✏️ **Read and circle.**

1 This is my mum.
She's a dancer.

a   b

2 This is my aunt.
She's a cook.

a   b

3 This is my sister.
She's six.

a   b

9 ✏️✏️ **Write. Then colour.**

1 _____

2 _____

3 _____

4 _____

5 _____

6 _____

mum
dad
brother
sister
granny
grandad
me

10 🖊 Read the words and circle.

~~can~~ cap dig dog

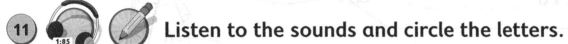

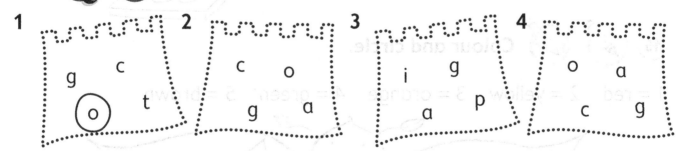

11 🎧 1:85 🖊 Listen to the sounds and circle the letters.

1 g c ⓞ t

2 c o g a

3 i g a p

4 o a c g

12 🎧 1:86 🖊 Listen and write the letters.   c g o

1 C   **2** ___   **3** ___

13 🎧 1:87 🖊 Listen and write the words.

1 g a s   **2** ___   **3** ___   **4** ___

14   **Read and write.**

drawing   sculpture   ~~painting~~   collage

1 It's a _painting_ .

2 It's a _____ .

3 It's a _____ .

4 It's a _____ .

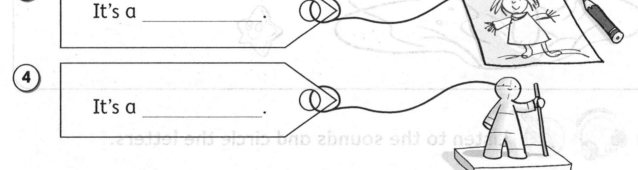

15  **Colour and circle.**

1 = red   2 = yellow   3 = orange   4 = green   5 = brown

It's a (drawing / sculpture). It's a (bird / butterfly).

3

16 1:91 **Look and draw. Then listen and number.**

a

b

c

1

d

17 **Complete for you. Then ask a classmate.**

	me	classmate
How old are you?		
What's your mum's name?		
What's your brother's / sister's / friend's name?		
How old is your brother / sister / friend?		

18   **Listen. Circle *True* or *False*.**

1 (True)/ False

2 True / False

3 True / False

4 True / False

5 True / False

19  **Look at Activity 18. Read and circle.**

1 This is my ((mum) / dad).
She's a (vet / (pilot)).
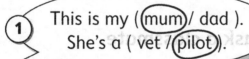

2 This is my (dad / grandad).
He's a (doctor / farmer).

3 This is my (sister / brother).
(His / Her) name's Rita.
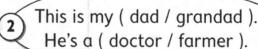

4 This is my (sister / brother).
(He's / She's) four.

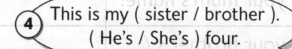

5 This is (Amy / Rita).
(He's / She's) my friend.
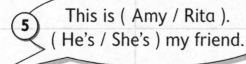

20 **Read and write.**

mum ~~dad~~ brother

This is my family. This is my

¹ **dad**. He's a doctor.

His name's Paul.

My ² _____ is a vet.

Her name's Alice.

And this is my ³ _____.

He's two! His name's Sam.

21   **Draw one person in your family and write.**

This is my

_____.

He's / She's a

_____.

His / Her name's

_____.

4 My body

1 **Look and write.**

~~head~~ feet leg hand body fingers arm

1 head

2 _____

3 _____

4 _____

5 _____

6 _____

7 _____

Read. Then circle.

1 foot      

2 wings      

3 hand         

4 arms      

3 **Listen and circle. Then colour.**

1 I've got a (pink / purple) body.

2 I've got (brown / orange) hands.

3 I've got (yellow / blue) feet.

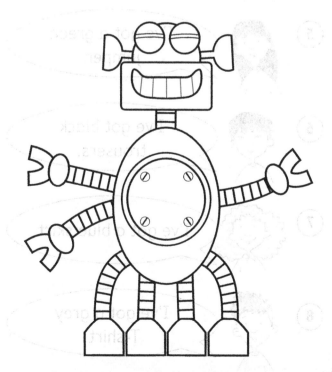

4 **Read and match. Then write and colour.**

socks   skirt   T-shirt   hat
dress   jumper   trousers   ~~shoes~~

1 I've got brown shoes.

a  _____

2 I've got a pink hat.

b  _____

3 I've got a red dress.

c  _____

4 I've got purple socks.

d  shoes

5 I've got a green jumper.

e  _____

6 I've got black trousers.

f  _____

7 I've got a blue skirt.

g  _____

8 I've got a grey T-shirt.

h 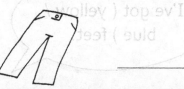 _____

5   **Count and write. Then colour.**

~~one~~　six　four　eight　one

1 She's got _one_ head. It's red.

2 She's got _____ arms. They're black.

3 She's got _____ feet. They're blue.

4 She's got _____ toes. They're yellow.

5 She's got _____ body. It's green.

6  **Follow. Then choose and write.**

 ①

 ②

③

④

 ⓐ

ⓑ

ⓒ

ⓓ

1 (He's) / She's got a ___hat___ .

2 He's / She's got a _____ .

3 He's / She's got _____ .

4 He's / She's got _____ .

| trousers |
| dress |
| ~~hat~~ |
| socks |

7 Draw. Then ✔ or ✗ and write correct sentences.

four	two	four

1 I've got five heads. ☐

I've got _____ heads.

2 I've got three arms. ☐

I've got _____ arms.

3 I've got two legs. ☐

I've got _____ legs.

8 Look and ✔ = clean or ✗ = not clean.

1

2

42 Lesson 5

9 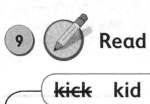 Read the words and circle.

~~kick~~ kid neck sock

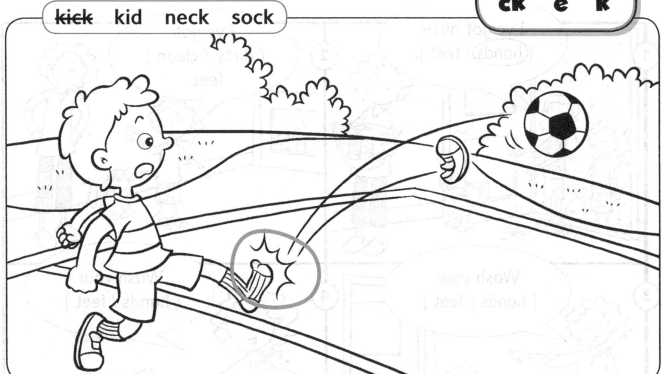

10  Listen to the sounds and circle the letters.

1 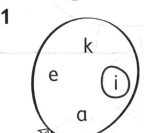   **2** 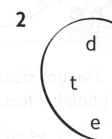   **3** 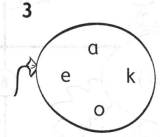   **4**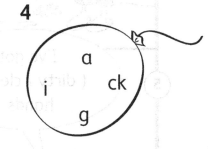

11  Listen and write the letters.   ck e ~~k~~

1 __k__   **2** ____   **3** ____

12   Listen and write the words.

1 k i t   **2** ____   **3** ____   **4** ____

13 **Read and circle.**

14 **Listen and check your answers.**

Wider World

15 **Read and match.**

①

②

③

ⓐ I'm a bird.

ⓑ I'm a butterfly.

ⓒ I'm a dinosaur.

16  **Choose a carnival costume. Colour and write.**

a dress	wings
a mask	a hat
trousers	
a T-shirt	

This is my carnival costume.

I've got _____ and _____.

17   **Read and circle. Then colour.**

1   I've got a (body / foot).

(It's / They're) green.

2   I've got three (finger / fingers).

(It's / They're) pink.

3   I've got five (leg / legs).

(It's / They're) brown.

4   I've got (feet / foot).

(It's / They're) orange.

18 **Look and ✓ or ✗.**

1   He's got a clean T-shirt.   ✗

2   She's got a dirty dress.   ☐

3   He's got dirty shoes.   ☐

4   She's got clean shoes.   ☐

19   **Read and write. Then colour.**

arms   eight   ~~head~~   three

This is my monster. He's got one ¹ __head__ . It's yellow.

He's got a green body.

He's got two ² _____.
They're pink. And he's got
³ _____ purple fingers.

He's got three legs. They're blue.
And he's got ⁴ _____ black feet.

He's got a green hat.

His name's Spike!

20 **Draw a monster and write.**

This is my monster.

He's got one _____.

It's _____.

He's got _____.

They're _____.

He's got _____.

They're _____ His name's

_____!

5 Pets

 1 **Look and write.**

frog	cat	dog	hamster	mouse
~~parrot~~	rabbit	snake	tortoise	

1

parrot

2

3

4

5

6

7

8

9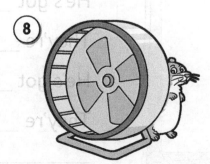

2 **Find and circle.**

1 a snake **2** two frogs **3** a parrot **4** a tortoise **5** three mice

3 **Look at Activity 2. Read and circle.**

1 (What's that?) / What are those?   (It's a snake.) / They're snakes.

2 What's that? / What are those?   It's a frog. / They're frogs.

3 What's that? / What are those?   It's a parrot. / They're parrots.

4 What's that? / What are those?   It's a tortoise. / They're tortoises.

5 What's that? / What are those?   It's a mouse. / They're mice.

4 **Look and write.**

 young ~~small~~ thin old
tall fat big short

①

②

③

④

small _____

⑤

⑥

⑦

⑧

_____ _____

5 **Look and write.** frog ~~rabbit~~ cat dog

1 He's got a rabbit . 2 She's _____.

3 _____ . 4 _____.

①

②

③

④

6 Listen, look and ✓.

1 Yes, he has. ✓

No, he hasn't. ☐

3 Yes, he has. ☐

No, he hasn't. ☐

5 Yes, he has. ☐

No, he hasn't. ☐

2 Yes, she has. ☐

No, she hasn't. ☐

4 Yes, she has. ☐

No, she hasn't. ☐

6 Yes, she has. ☐

No, she hasn't. ☐

7 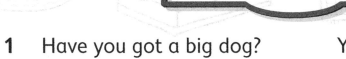 Read and circle about your pets.

1	Have you got a big dog?	Yes, I have. / No, I haven't.
2	Have you got a small rabbit?	Yes, I have. / No, I haven't.
3	Have you got a fat cat?	Yes, I have. / No, I haven't.
4	Have you got a long snake?	Yes, I have. / No, I haven't.
5	Have you got an old hamster?	Yes, I have. / No, I haven't.

8 **Listen and number.**

9 **Who lives here? Look and match.**

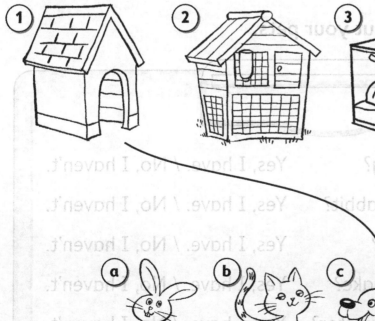

10 ✏️ Read the words and circle.

~~bag~~   cup   hat   rat

11 🎧 2:45 ✏️ **Listen to the sounds and circle the letters.**

1   2   3   4

(teapot 1: r, n, b, ⓗ)   (teapot 2: h, u, r, b)   (teapot 3: b, a, r, u)   (teapot 4: n, h, b, p)

12 🎧 2:46 ✏️ **Listen and write the letters.**   b   h   r   u

1 r   2 ____   3 ____   4 ____

13 🎧 2:47 ✏️ **Listen and write the words.**

1 u p   2 ____   3 ____   4 ____

14 **Write. Then match.**

chick   kitten   puppy

1   **2**   **3**

_____

15 **Join the dots. Then read and circle.**

It's a (kitten / puppy / chick).   It's a (kitten / puppy / chick).

16 Follow and write. | rat   tortoise   ~~spider~~

1  I've got a **spider** .

2  I've got a _____ .

3  I've got a _____ .

a

b

c

17 Look at Activity 16 and write.

Yes, I have
No, I haven't

1  Have you got a snake? _____ .

2   Have you got a spider? _____ .

18 Read and answer.

1 Have you got an unusual pet? _____ .

2 What pet have you got? _____ .

Lesson 8   55

19 Read and answer.

| Yes, he has | No, he hasn't |
| Yes, she has | No, she hasn't |

1 Has he got a dog?

Yes, he has _____.

2 Has she got a rabbit?

_____.

3 Has he got a parrot?

_____.

4 Has she got a frog?

_____.

20 Read and match. Then write.

| thin   small   ~~old~~   long   young   ~~fat~~ |

1 What's that?

It's a dog. It's ___ old ___ and ___ fat ___.

2 What are those?

They're snakes. They're _____ and _____.

3 What are those?

They're kittens. They're _____ and _____.

21   **Read and circle. Then colour.**

ABOUT ME

I've got a **¹**(puppy / kitten).

He's **²**(small / big) and orange.

He's got **³**(two / four) legs.

He's got a **⁴**(long / short) tail.

⁵(His / Her) name's Minty.

22   **Draw a pet and write.**

I've got a _____.

He's / She's _____ and

_____.

He's / She's got _____ legs.

He's / She's got a

_____ tail.

His / Her name's _____.

6 My house

1  **Draw. Then write.**

bathroom	bedroom	garden	door
kitchen	living room	~~window~~

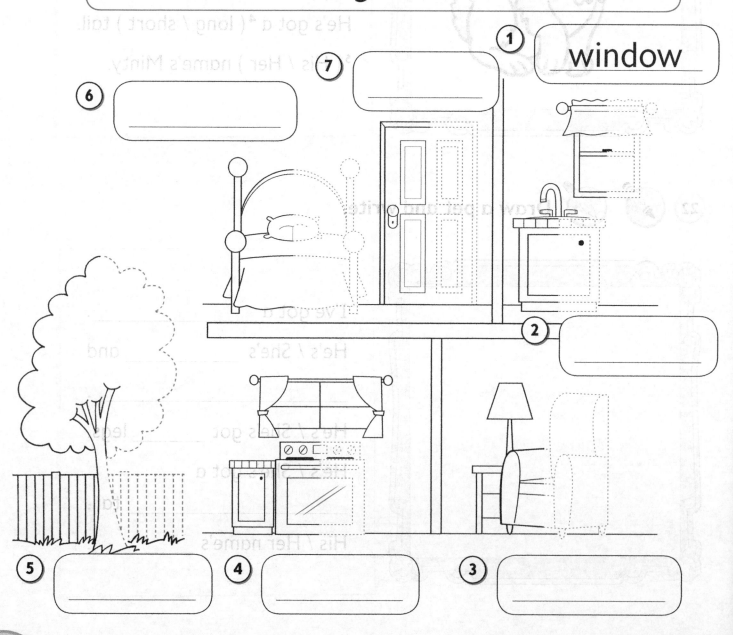

1 __window__

Listen and number. Then read and match.

She's in the bathroom.

He's in the garden.

They're in the kitchen.

They're in the living room.

1

 Join the dots. Then read and circle.

(Where's / Where are) Waldo?

He's in the (kitchen / living room).

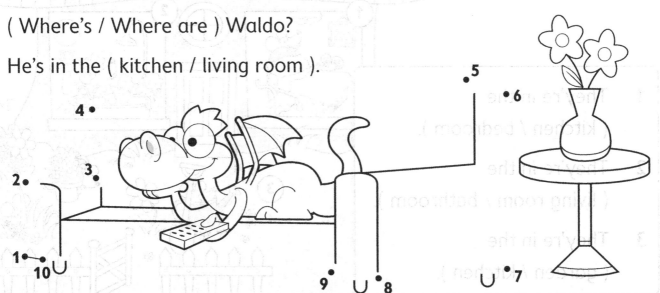

 **4** **Listen and number. Then write.**

fridge   bath   sink
TV   sofa   bed
cooker   lamp

a  ☐

b  **1**

c 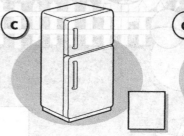 ☐

d  ☐

e  ☐

f  ☐

g  ☐

h  ☐

5 **Look, read and circle.**

1 They're in the
(kitchen / bedroom).

2 They're in the
(living room / bathroom).

3 They're in the
(garden / kitchen).

6   **Read and find. Then circle and write.**

| under   in   on |

1   (**There's** / There are) a bird __under__ the window.

2   (There's / There are) two rabbits _____ the fridge.

3   (There's / There are) a teddy _____ the bath.

4   (There's / There are) two dogs _____ the table.

5   (There's / There are) books _____ the bed.

6   (There's / There are) a boy _____ the sofa.

7   (There's / There are) a cat _____ the bed.

7 Listen and ✓ or ✗.

8 Look and match.

MY BEDROOM

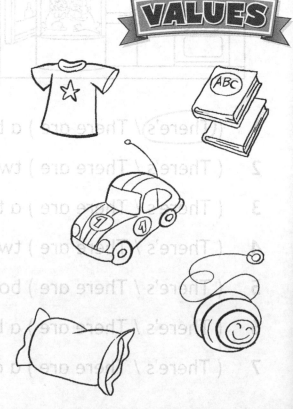

9 ✏️ Read the words and circle.

~~bell~~ doll fan leg

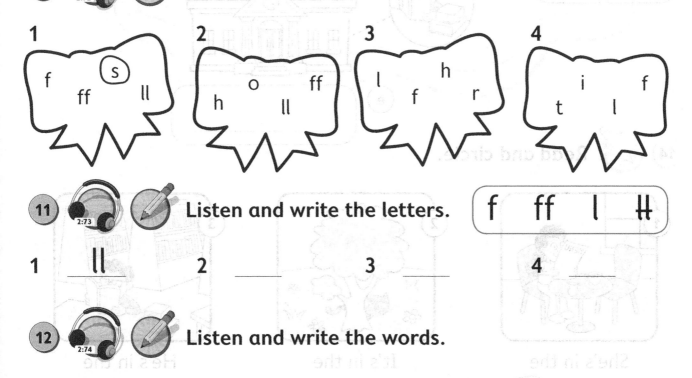

PHONICS

f ff l ll

10 🎧 2:72 ✏️ Listen to the sounds and circle the letters.

1 f ff (s) ll

2 o ff h ll

3 l h f r

4 i f t l

11 🎧 2:73 ✏️ Listen and write the letters.

f ff l ~~ll~~

1 ll   2 _____   3 ___   4 ___

12 🎧 2:74 ✏️ Listen and write the words.

1 ___   2 _____   3 _____   4 ___

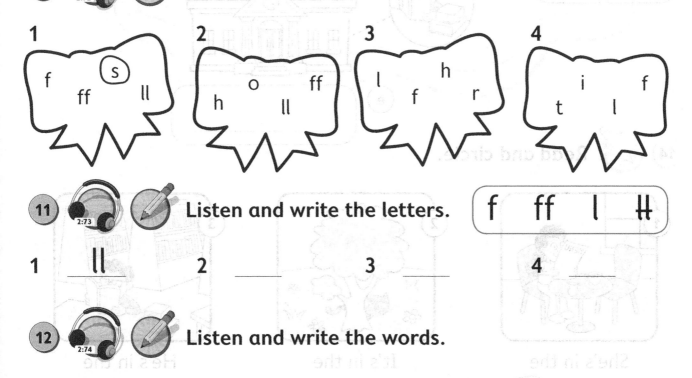

13   2:77 **Write. Then listen and follow the path.**

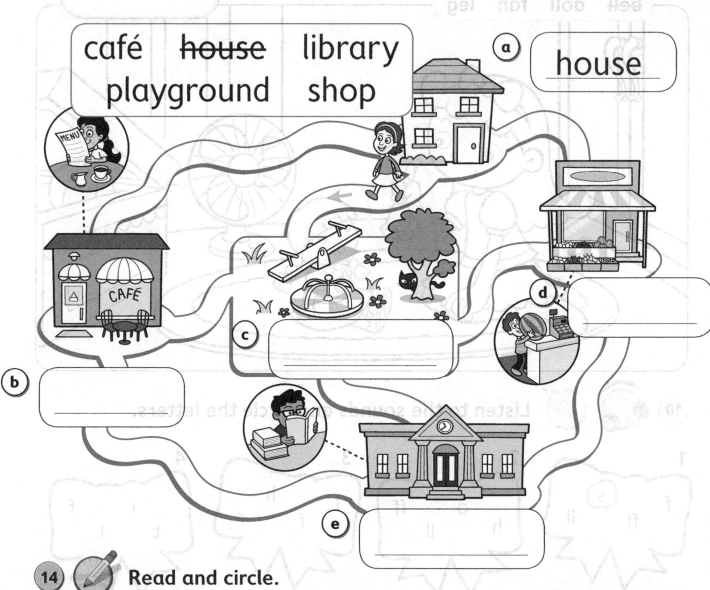

café ~~house~~ library
playground shop

a house

b
c
d
e

14 **Read and circle.**

1

She's in the
(playground / café).

2

It's in the
(shop / park).

3

He's in the
(library / café).

Wider World

15 **Read and match.**

1

2

3

4

a   flat

b   caravan

c   houseboat

d   house

16  **Read and complete the letter.**

cat ~~house~~ bed
living room   bedroom
kitchen   TV   bedrooms
bathroom   garden

Hi! My name's Ella.

I live in a small  ¹ __house__ .

There's a ² _____, a  ³ _____,

a ⁴ _____ and two  ⁵ _____.

And there's a big ⁶ _____.

My favourite room is my  ⁷ _____.

I've got a big ⁸ _____ and a  ⁹ _____.

And I've got a ¹⁰ _____! Her name's Cleo.

Goodbye!

Listen and draw.

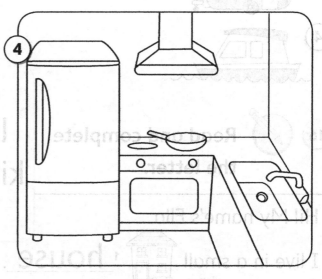

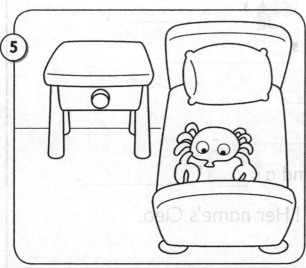

18 **Read and write.**

lamp ~~bedroom~~ chairs big two

My favourite room is my
¹ bedroom .

It's ² _____ .

There are ³ _____ beds
and two ⁴ _____ .

There's a table.

There's a ⁵ _____ on
the table.

I've got a TV.

19   **Draw your favourite room and write.**

My favourite room is my

_____ .

It's _____ .

There's _____ .

There are _____ .

I've got a _____ .

7 Food

 **Draw. Then write.**

bread	cake	cheese
fish	fruit	milk
salad	yoghurt	

(1)

_____

(2)

_____

(3)

_____

(4)

_____

(5)

_____

(6)

_____

(7)

_____

(8)

_____

Find and colour. Then ✓ or ✗.

(2)

salad ☐

fish ☐

yoghurt ☐

fruit ☐

bread ☐

milk ☐

cheese ☐

cake ☐

I like...

(3) **Read and draw.**

I like fish and salad. I don't like cheese.

I like juice.

4 ✏️ **Look and number.**

honey	☐	ice cream	☐	water	1	vegetables	☐
jelly	☐	chocolate	☐	sandwich	☐	meat	☐

5 🎧 3:10 ✏️ **Listen and number. Then circle and write.**

a   b   c   d

1   I ((like) / don't like) ___honey___ .

2   I (like / don't like) _____ .

3   _____ .

4   _____ .

cheese
~~honey~~
jelly
meat

6 🎧 3:14 ✏️ **Listen and number.**

a

b

c

d

1

7 ✏️ **Look and write.**

1 Do you like jelly?

_____, I _____.

2 Do you like honey?

_____, I _____.

8 ✏️ **Read and match.**

1 I like apples.
2 I like ice cream.

a
b
c HONEY
d

9 🎧 3:16 ✏️ **Listen and number.**

a
b 1
c
d

10 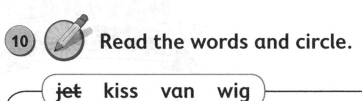 Read the words and circle.

jet   kiss   van   wig

11  Listen to the sounds and circle the letters.

1
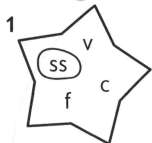
v
ss   c
f

2

w
o   u
v

3

j
v   i
w

4
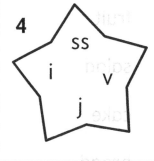
ss
i   v
j

12  Listen and write the letters.

 j   SS   V   W

1 ___W___   2 _____   3 _____   4 _____

13 Listen and write the words.

1 m e s s   2 _____   3 _____   4 _____

14 Follow and write.

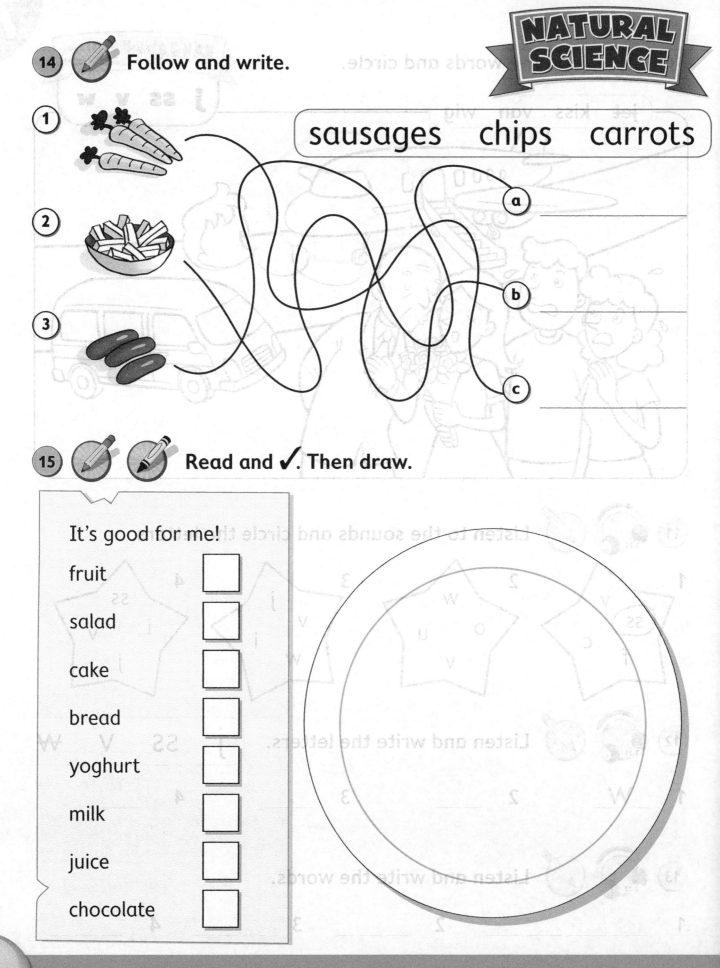

1

2

3

sausages   chips   carrots

a _____

b _____

c _____

15 Read and ✓. Then draw.

It's good for me!

fruit ☐

salad ☐

cake ☐

bread ☐

yoghurt ☐

milk ☐

juice ☐

chocolate ☐

Wider World

16 🎧 3:25 ✏️ **What has Ella got? Listen and ✓.**

meat	✓	vegetables	☐
fish	☐	salad	☐
fruit	☐	water	☐
ice cream	☐	juice	☐
yoghurt	☐	milk	☐

17 ✏️ **What have you got? Ask a classmate and ✓.**

meat	☐	vegetables	☐
fish	☐	salad	☐
fruit	☐	water	☐
ice cream	☐	juice	☐
yoghurt	☐	milk	☐

18 3:26   **Listen, draw and write.**

| I like | ~~I don't like~~ | I like | I don't like |

①

I don't like salad.

②

③

④

_____
_____ .

_____
_____ .

_____
_____ .

19 **Read. Then look and write.**

| Yes, I do |
| No, I don't |

① Do you like milk?   **Yes, I do** . ☺

② Do you like juice?   _____ . ☹

③ Do you like meat?   _____ . ☺

20 **Read and circle.**

I ¹(like / don't like) meat and chips.

I ²(like / don't like) fruit. My favourite food is ³(pizza / salad).

I ⁴(like / don't like) sausages.

21   **Draw your favourite food and write.**

I like _____ and

_____ .

I don't like _____ .

My favourite food is

_____ .

8 I'm happy!

1 Look and write.

| happy | hungry | scared | thirsty | tired |

1

I'm _____ .

2

I'm _____ .

3

I'm _____ .

4

I'm _____ .

5

I'm _____ .

 **Listen and circle.**

1 (Yes, I am.)/
No, I'm not.

2 Yes, I am. /
No, I'm not.

3 Yes, I am. /
No, I'm not.

4 Yes, I am. /
No, I'm not.

 Find. Then read and circle.

1 She's (happy / tired).

2 He's (thirsty / tired).

3 He's (happy / thirsty).

4 She's (scared / hungry).

5 He's (happy / hungry).

4 **Look and write.**

> angry   bored   cold
> ~~happy~~   hot   hurt
> sad   ill

1 She's __happy__ .   **2** He's _____ .   **3** She's _____ .   **4** He's _____ .

5 She's _____ .   **6** He's _____ .   **7** She's _____ .   **8** He's _____ .

5   **Read and answer the questions. Then draw yourself.**

> Yes, I am   No, I'm not

1 Are you happy? _____ .

2 Are you cold? _____ .

3 Are you angry? _____ .

4 Are you bored? _____ .

5 Are you hungry? _____ .

6   **Listen and number.**

7 **Look. Then circle and write.**

1

Are you happy?

Yes, I am. / (No, I'm not.)

I'm _sad_ .

2

Are they hot?

Yes, they are. / No, they aren't.

They're _____.

3

Is she bored?

Yes, she is. / No, she isn't.

She's _____.

4

Is he tired?

Yes, he is. / No, he isn't.

He's _____.

9 **Look and write.**

hurt   help   sad

Are you _____ ?   Are you _____ ?   Can I _____ you?

10 Read the words and circle.

PHONICS

qu   x   y
z   zz

~~box~~   buzz   taxi   yes

Yes!

TAXI

11  Listen to the sounds and circle the letters.

1
z y
x j

2
x
z y
zz

3
qu
ck
zz y

4
w
x qu
ck

12  Listen and write the letters.   qu X y z̶ ZZ

1 __Z__   2 _____   3 _____   4 _____   5 _____

13 Listen and write the words.

1 q u i z   2 _____   3 _____   4 _____

14  **Look and match.**

1

It's hot.

2

It's cold.

3

4

15 **Look and circle.**

1

2

It's a (polar bear / penguin).   It's a (turtle / snake).

It's (hot / cold).   It's (hot / cold).

Wider World

16 **Read and match. Then circle.**

1

2

a I'm Anna. I live in Florida. It's (hot / cold) here. I like the (sea / snow).

b My name is Ben. I live in Alaska. It's (hot / cold) here. I like the (sea / snow).

17   **What about you? Draw and write.**

My name is _____.

I live in _____.

It's _____ here.

I like the _____.

18 Write.

angry   bored   cold
hot   hungry   hurt
ill   thirsty

1

Are you _____?

Yes, I am.

2

Is he _____?

Yes, he is.

3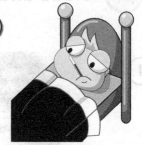

Is he bored?

No, he isn't.

He's _____.

4

Is she _____?

Yes, she is.

5

Is he _____?

Yes, he is.

6

Are you hot?

No, I'm not.

I'm _____.

7

Is she _____?

Yes, she is.

8

Is he cold?

No, he isn't.

He's _____.

19   **Read and circle. Then colour.**

This is me on my birthday.
I'm ¹(happy / sad).

I've got ²(three / five) balloons.
They're red, green and blue.
And I'm ³(hungry / thirsty).

I've got a ⁴(big / small)
chocolate cake!

20   **Draw yourself on your birthday and write.**

This is me on my birthday.

I'm _____.

I've got _____ balloons.

They're _____.

I'm _____.

I've got a _____
birthday cake!

Goodbye

1 **Look and write.**

apple   balloon   bird   cake
door   hat   photo   tablet   teddy

①

②

③

_____

④

⑤

⑥

_____

⑦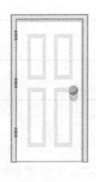

⑧

⑨

_____

3:56 **Listen and number.**

a ☐   b ☐   c ☐

d ☐   e ☐   f ☐

g ☐   h ☐   i ☐

3 **Look and write.**

1

We like

_____.

2

I've got two

_____.

3

This is my pet.

It's a _____.

4

Do you like

_____?

Yes, I do.

4 ✏️ **Look, circle and write.**

1 Is it a cat?

(Yes / No), it _____ .

2 Is it a pencil?

(Yes / No), it _____ .

3 Is it a head?

(Yes / No), it _____ .

4 Is it a cake?

(Yes / No), it _____ .

5 Is it a cooker?

(Yes / No), it _____ .

6 Is it a jumper?

(Yes / No), it _____ .

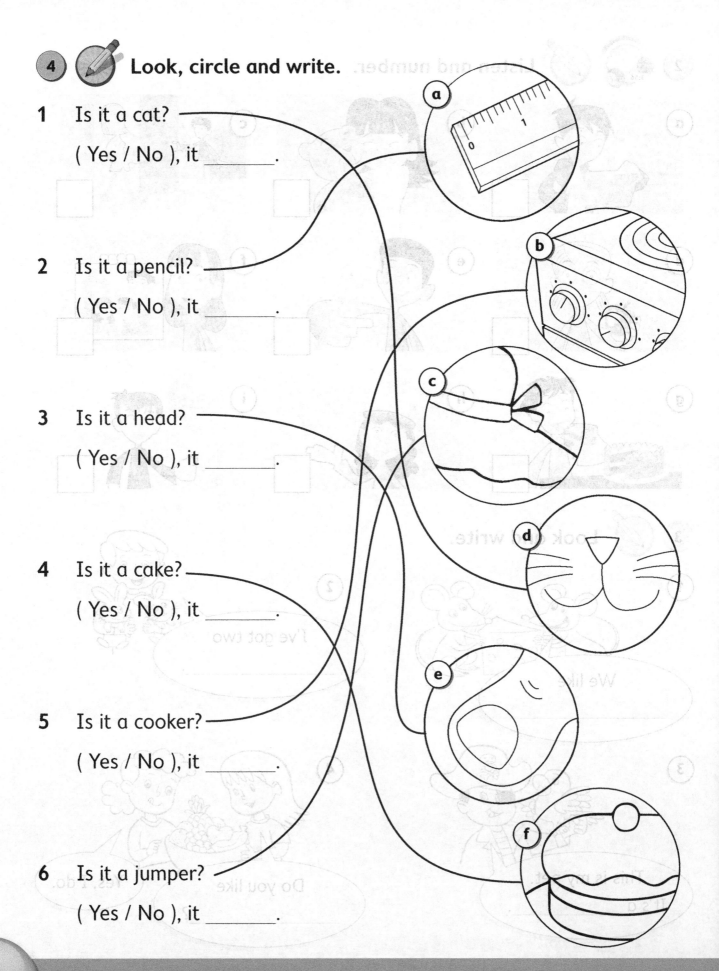

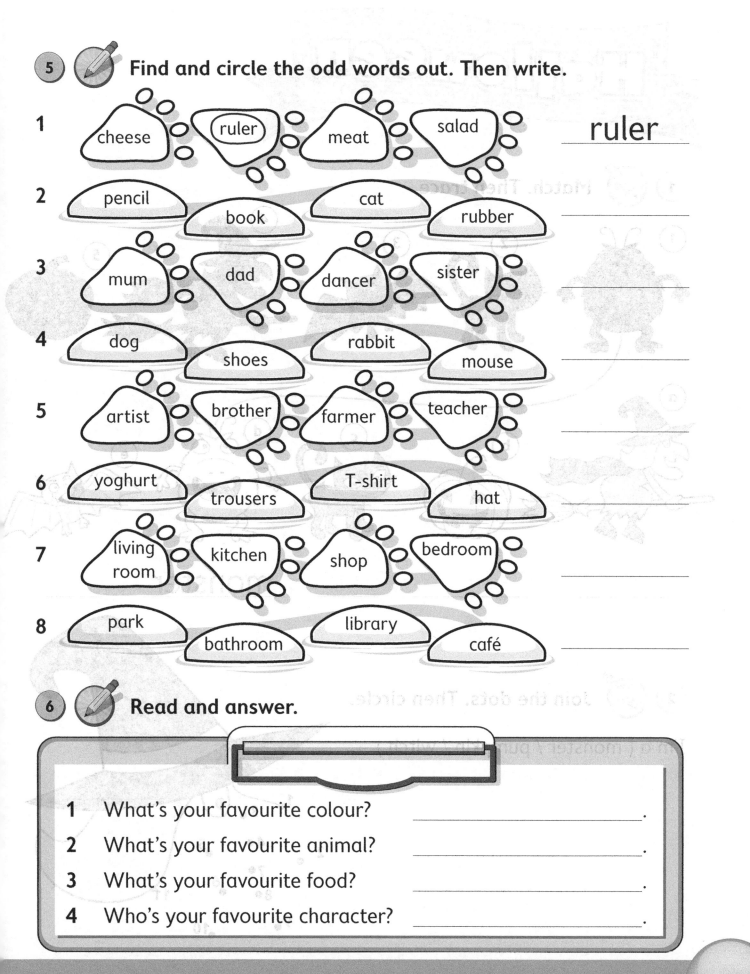

5 Find and circle the odd words out. Then write.

1 cheese (ruler) meat salad   ruler

2 pencil book cat rubber   _____

3 mum dad dancer sister   _____

4 dog shoes rabbit mouse   _____

5 artist brother farmer teacher   _____

6 yoghurt trousers T-shirt hat   _____

7 living room kitchen shop bedroom   _____

8 park bathroom library café   _____

6 Read and answer.

1 What's your favourite colour? _____.

2 What's your favourite animal? _____.

3 What's your favourite food? _____.

4 Who's your favourite character? _____.

Halloween

1 ✏ **Match. Then trace.**

witch   pumpkin   cat   monster   bat

2 ✏ **Join the dots. Then circle.**

I'm a (monster / pumpkin / witch).

Christmas

1  **Trace and match. Then listen and colour.**

a sleigh **b** present **c** reindeer **d** Santa

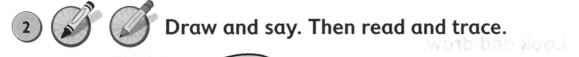

2 **Draw and say. Then read and trace.**

To _____,
Happy _____
Christmas!
From Santa.

Easter

1 **Colour and write.** | chick · egg · ~~bunny~~

 bunny

 _____

 _____

It's an _____ .

2 **Look and draw.**

①   

②   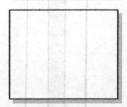

③   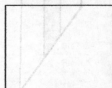

Summer fun

1 🖊 **Read and match.**

① (sun)   **②** (sky)   **③** (tree)

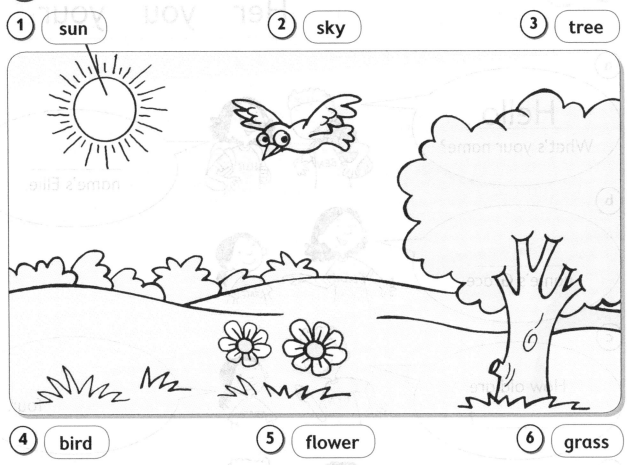

④ (bird)   **⑤** (flower)   **⑥** (grass)

2 🖊🖊 **Choose and write. Then colour the picture in Activity 1.**

~~blue~~ brown purple yellow green red

The sky is ___blue___ . The sun is _____ .

The tree is _____ . The bird is _____ .

The flowers are _____ . The grass is _____ .

Extra practice

1 Choose and write.

My	Yes	~~Hello~~	I'm	it
Her	you	your	is	

a

Hello . What's your name?

_____ name's Ellie.

b

_____ name's Grace.

c

How old are _____?

_____ four.

d

What's _____ favourite colour?

My favourite colour _____ blue.

e

What's your favourite colour? Is _____ blue?

_____, it is.

1 **Choose and write.**

it	these	~~this~~	blue
pencils	They're	many	
they	book	Three	

a

What's _**this**_ ?

It's a _____.

b

Is _____ red?

No, it isn't. It's blue. It's a _____ book.

c

What are _____ ?

They're _____.

d

What colour are _____ ?

_____ purple.

e

How _____ pencils can you see?

_____.

1   **Choose and write.**

| this | Is | ~~He's~~ | She's |
| my | No | she | |

a This is my brother. <u>He's</u> ten.

b And _____ is my sister.

How old is _____ ?

c _____ five.

d This is _____ mum.

_____ she a dentist?

e _____, she isn't. She's a vet.

1 **Choose and write.**

He's I've ~~got~~ They're

a

He's __got__ a blue head and a red body.

b

_____ got four arms. They're green.

c

He's got three legs. _____ blue.

d

_____ got a red head and a green body. I've got blue feet.

5

 1 **Choose and write.**

are	It's	They're	long	you
Has	~~What's~~	hasn't	I've	

a

__What's__ that?

_____ a big cat.

b

What _____ those?

_____ rats.

c

_____ she got a rat?

No, she _____. She's got a hamster.

d

Have _____ got a rat?

No, I haven't. _____ got a snake.

It's a _____ snake!

1 **Choose and write.**

| are Where's under There's |
| She's They're ~~Where~~ |

a

Where are Mum and Dad?

_____ in the living room.

b

Where's Grace?

_____ in the bedroom.

c

Hmm. _____ a lamp on the desk.
There _____ two rabbits on the bed.

_____ Grace?

d

She's _____ the bed.

7

Yes	Thank	~~like~~	don't	Do	you

a

I ___like___ sandwiches and fruit.
I _____ like meat.

b

_____ you like meat, Grace?

_____, I do.
I like meat. I don't like sandwiches!

c

Here _____ are.

d

_____ you!

Choose and write.

Are	you	they	~~I'm~~
am	He's	he	Thank

a I'm thirsty.

And __I'm__ hungry?

b Are _____ hungry?

Yes, I _____ .

c Is _____ hungry?

No, he isn't. _____ thirsty.

d Here you are.

_____ you.

e _____ they happy?

Yes, _____ are.

Unit 8 Extra practice 103

Picture dictionary

Unit 1

 My birthday

red   yellow   green   blue   pink   purple   orange   brown   black   white   grey

 Numbers

one   two   three   four   five   six   seven   eight   nine   ten

 **Actions**

jump   walk   stamp   clap   run   dance   climb   hop

 **Natural Science**

            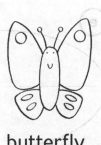

bird   fish   flower   leaf   butterfly

Unit 2

Classroom objects

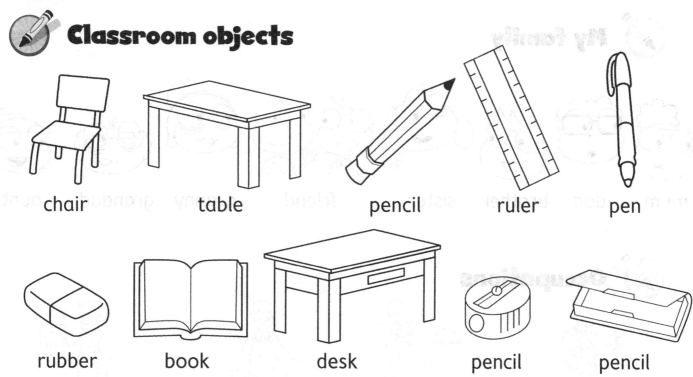

chair   table   pencil   ruler   pen

rubber   book   desk   pencil sharpener   pencil case

Numbers

eleven   twelve   thirteen   fourteen   fifteen

sixteen   seventeen   eighteen   nineteen   twenty

Music

guitar   piano   violin   drum

Unit 3

 My family

mum   dad   brother   sister   friend   granny   grandad   aunt

 Occupations

doctor   cook   vet   dentist

pilot   artist   dancer   farmer   teacher

 Art

 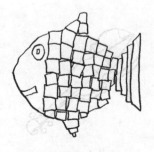  

painting   collage   drawing   sculpture

Unit 4

My body

head

arms

feet

hands

body

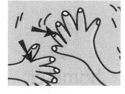
fingers

legs

toes

wings

tail

 ## Clothes

T-shirt

jumper

trousers

dress

skirt

shoes

socks

hat

 ## Natural Science

clean hands

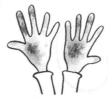
dirty hands

a dirty face

wash your hands

Unit 5

 Pets

dog

cat

rabbit

parrot

mouse

tortoise

frog

snake

hamster

 Adjectives

big

small

tall

short

long

thin

fat

young

old

 Natural Science

chick

kitten

puppy

egg

goose

bird

Unit 6

 At home (1)

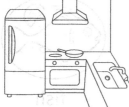

kitchen

living room

door

garden

bathroom

bedroom

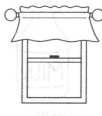

window

house

 At home (2)

bath

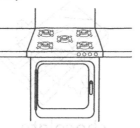

cooker

fridge

TV

sofa

lamp

bed

sink

 Social Science

shop

library

playground

café

park

Unit 7

 Food (1)

cake

fruit

bread

cheese

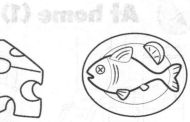
fish

yoghurt

milk

juice

salad

 Food (2)

sandwich

water

chocolate

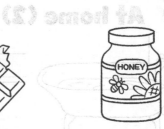
honey

jelly

vegetables

ice cream

meat

 Natural Science

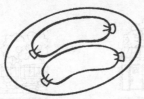
sausages

chips

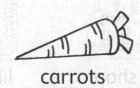
carrots

Unit 8

Adjectives (1)

| happy | scared | tired | hungry | thirsty |

Adjectives (2)

| sad | hot | cold | ill | hurt | angry | bored |

 Natural Science

It's hot.

It's cold.

Pearson Education Limited
Edinburgh Gate
Harlow
Essex CM20 2JE
England
and Associated Companies throughout the world.

Poptropica® English Islands

© Pearson Education Limited 2017

Editorial and project management by hyphen

First published 2017
ISBN: 978-1-2921-9802-6
Fifth impression 2019

Set in Fiendstar 17/21pt
Printed in Malaysia (CTP-VVP)

Acknowledgements: The publisher would like to thank Tessa Lochowski, Steve Elsworth and Jim Rose for their contributions to this edition.

Illustrators: Chan Siu Fai, Moreno Chiacchiera (Beehive Illustration), Adam Clay, Leo Cultura, Andrew Hennessey, James Horvath (Beehive Illustration), Marek Jagucki, Sue King, Stephenine Lau, Daniel Limon (Beehive Illustration), Katie McDee, Bill McGuire (Shannon Associates), Jackie Stafford, Olimpia Wong and Yam Wai Lun

Picture Credits: The publisher would like to thank the following for their kind permission to reproduce their photographs:
(Key: b-bottom; c-centre; l-left; r-right; t-top)

Shutterstock.com: forden 85l, Svitlana-ua 85r

Cover images: *Back:* **Fotolia.com:** frender r; **Shutterstock.com:** Denys Prykhodov l

All other images © Pearson Education

Every effort has been made to trace the copyright holders and we apologize in advance for any unintentional omissions. We would be pleased to insert the appropriate acknowledgement in any subsequent edition of this publication.